Why Does My Cat ROAR?

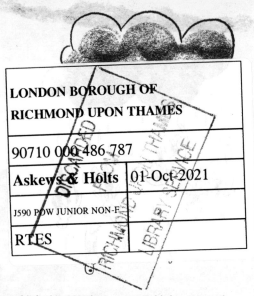

This edition published in 2021 by Arcturus Publishing Limited
26/27 Bickels Yard, 151–153 Bermondsey Street,
London SE1 3HA

Illustrator: Luke Séguin-Magee
Authors: Marc Powell and William Potter
Editors: Susie Rae and Joe Harris
Designer: Rosie Bellwood

CH007049NT
Supplier: 10, Date 0621, Print run 11573

Printed in the UK

MIX
Paper from
responsible sources
FSC® C018072
www.fsc.org

CONTENTS

LET'S GO WILD!

Are you fascinated by the wonders of the natural world? Do you love all things furry, feathery, scaly, big, and small?

THEN PREPARE TO BE AMAZED, SHOCKED, OR TOTALLY GROSSED OUT BY THE HUNDREDS OF ANIMAL FACTS THAT FOLLOW.

Fangs, claws, frightful feasts, predators, parasites, and lots and lots of dung—it's all in here. Just be glad this is not a scratch and sniff book!

CRAZY CREATURES

HOW STRONG ARE RATS?

Rats are so tough that they can fall from the fifth floor of a building and walk away unharmed.

DID YOU KNOW?

Rats' teeth are so strong that they can bite through wood, metal, and electric cables. Not good news if they're in your attic, then!

HOW LONG DO A RAT'S TEETH GROW?

A rat's teeth grow continuously during its life. If it didn't keep chewing, its lower teeth would eventually grow through its top jaw and through the roof of its mouth.

CAN RATS SWIM?

Rats can tread water for three days and swim for 0.8km (half a mile) without a rest.

DO RAT TAILS GET TANGLED?

Rats that hibernate together sometimes get their tails tied up in a big knot. If the rats urinate over themselves in the winter, they can freeze together in a block!

HOW MANY BABIES DO RATS HAVE?

In just 18 months, two rats can have between 2-3 million babies.

HOW MUCH BLOOD DO VAMPIRE BATS DRINK?

A vampire bat can drink half its own body weight in blood every day.

HOW MUCH FRUIT DO FRUIT BATS EAT?

A plague of flying foxes (fruit bats) has been known to consume an entire orchard in just one night!

DID YOU KNOW?

Vampire bats are surprisingly thoughtful. If a bat is too ill to go out and feed, another bat will suck blood all night, come home, and vomit it over the sick bat so that it doesn't miss out on a meal. How kind!

HOW MANY BUGS DO BATS EAT?

Just a single bat can eat between 3,000 and 7,000 mosquitoes in a night. A colony of 500 of the flying fiends can munch their way through a quarter of a million bugs in an hour.

WHAT USE IS BAT POOP?

Bracken Cave in Texas, USA, is home to 20 million bats. The floor is caked in a thick layer of bat feces that the locals collect to use as fertilizer.

DID YOU KNOW?

West African woolly bats are so small that they live in large spiderwebs.

WHY DOES A SKINK LOSE ITS TAIL?

The Polynesian skink (a small lizard) has a bright blue tail which it can shed if it is attacked. The tail continues wriggling after the lizard has gone, keeping the predator distracted.

DID YOU KNOW?

A chameleon can look in two directions at the same time because its eyes can move separately.

HOW DO CHAMELEONS CATCH BUGS?

Some chameleons have long tongues with a sticky, goo-covered lump on the end that they shoot out to snatch insects.

HOW MANY TEETH DOES AN ALLIGATOR HAVE?

An alligator can go through 3,000 teeth in its lifetime. Maybe somebody should teach them to brush properly!

DID YOU KNOW?

A crocodile can't stick out its tongue.

HOW DO CROCODILES EAT?

Crocodiles can't chew their food. Instead, they hold their prey and then twist their bodies and teeth around it to tear off chunks of flesh.

HOW MANY TEETH DOES AN ELEPHANT HAVE?

An elephant has four functional teeth, each one being 30cm (12 inches) long. They are replaced six times in a lifetime, but after the last replacement the elephant can no longer eat properly.

HOW CAREFUL IS AN ELEPHANT'S TRUNK?

As well as uprooting trees, an elephant's trunk can perform delicate operations such as plucking a single blade of grass from the ground.

DID YOU KNOW?

Elephants are right- or left-tusked, just like people can be right- or left-handed!

IS AN ELEPHANT A NOISY EATER?

An elephant's tummy makes so much noise when it's digesting food that if there's any danger of a predator hearing it, it can immediately stop digesting. Ingenious! Try it yourself!

DID YOU KNOW?

In 1916, an elephant was tried and hanged for murder in Erwin, Tennessee, USA.

HOW HIGH CAN AN ELEPHANT JUMP?

They can't! Elephants are some of the only mammals that can't jump.

IS THERE A FROG THAT'S SMALLER THAN ITS TADPOLE?

When it is a tadpole, the paradoxical frog of South America can grow to 25cm (10 inches), but then it shrinks to only 6cm (2.4in) when it becomes a fully grown frog!

WHAT IS THE ODDEST SOUND MADE BY A FROG?

In winter, the croak of a golden tree frog sounds like a mallet chipping away at a rock, but in summer, it sounds like a tinkling bell!

DID YOU KNOW?

Using a powerful magnet, it is possible to make a small frog lift off the ground and stay suspended in the air. Don't try it at home!

During mating competitions, Montana mountain goats can butt heads so hard that the shock can cause their hooves to fall off.

DID YOU KNOW?

Horns never stop growing but antlers are replaced every year.

DO ANIMALS SURF?

A fully grown moose was seen surfing down a river in 2006. The moose was spotted standing on a large chunk of ice and merrily making his way along the Namsen River in Norway.

HOW DO POLAR BEARS FIND FOOD?

Polar bears use their sense of smell to track down prey up to 30km (18 miles) away. Even thick ice doesn't stop them from tracking their prey.

DID YOU KNOW?

A polar bear's liver contains so much Vitamin A that it would be fatal if eaten by a human.

HOW BIG IS A POLAR BEAR'S BELLY?

The polar bear has the largest stomach capacity (in relation to its size) of any animal. It can kill and eat a large walrus or even a beluga whale.

IS A POLAR BEAR WHITE UNDER ITS FUR?

The skin under a polar bear's white fur is actually black!

DID YOU KNOW?

Polar bears are practically undetectable by infrared cameras because of their hollow fur.

HOW DO POLAR BEARS STOP THEIR FEET FROM GETTING COLD?

Polar bears are the only mammals with hair on the soles of their feet.

DO ALL ARCTIC ANIMALS HIBERNATE?

Arctic foxes don't. Unlike many other Arctic animals, they can stand temperatures as low as -50°C (-58°F).

IS A KOMODO DRAGON POISONOUS?

The bite of a Komodo dragon isn't poisonous, but there are so many bacteria in their mouths—growing in rotten meat between their teeth—that a bite from one often leads to blood poisoning and death.

HOW STRONG IS A GILA MONSTER BITE?

The bite of a Gila monster (a large venomous lizard) is so strong that the only way to detach one, once it has bitten, is to drown it.

WHAT IS THE WORLD'S FASTEST REPTILE?

The fastest reptile on the planet is the spiny-tailed iguana from Costa Rica, clocking in at a foot-burning 35km (22 miles) per hour.

DID YOU KNOW?

Shaving a pregnant mouse makes her produce more milk and grow larger babies. She becomes a "super mouse" because she can use more energy without overheating.

HOW DOES A POSSUM PLAY DEAD?

A possum "plays dead" if it feels threatened. It lies completely still, hangs its tongue out, leaks dung, and oozes green slime that smells like rotten flesh.

WHY AREN'T MEERKATS AFRAID OF SCORPIONS?

Meerkats are immune to many deadly types of venom and will eat scorpions, including their stingers.

WHAT'S THE BIGGEST THING A PYTHON CAN EAT?

A fully grown python can swallow a large pig—whole.

DID YOU KNOW?

The venomous copperhead snake smells like freshly cut cucumber. Just don't put one in your salad!

HOW OFTEN DOES A PYTHON NEED TO EAT?

A python can live for around six months without eating anything.

HOW DANGEROUS IS A KING COBRA'S VENOM?

The venom of the king cobra is so deadly that 1g (0.04oz) of it can kill 150 people. Just handling the substance with bare skin can put a person in a coma.

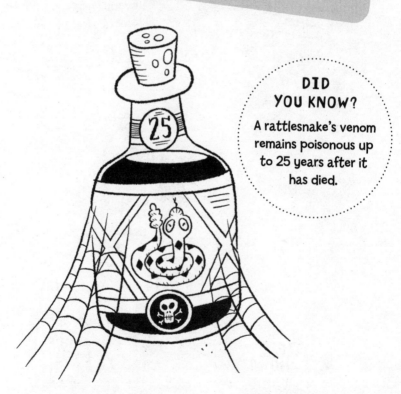

DID YOU KNOW?

A rattlesnake's venom remains poisonous up to 25 years after it has died.

WHICH SNAKE IS THE DEADLIEST?

Carpet vipers kill more people than any other type of snake; their bite leads to uncontrollable bleeding.

CAN ANY ANIMALS SURVIVE DRINKING POISON?

A porcupine can swallow 100 times the amount of poisonous hydrogen cyanide that is needed to kill a human—and suffer no ill effects.

IS A DUCKBILLED PLATYPUS A REAL ANIMAL?

Yes, but when staff at London's British Museum first saw one, they thought it was a fake animal and tried to pull off its bill!

DID YOU KNOW?

A kangaroo can't jump unless its tail is touching the ground.

HOW GOOD ARE ORANGUTANS AT SWINGING BETWEEN TREES?

Almost 50 percent of all orangutans have bone fractures due to regularly falling out of trees.

DID YOU KNOW?

The tarsier (a small primate) has eyes so large that it is the equivalent of a human having eyes the size of grapefruits!

WHAT'S THE SCARIEST-LOOKING ANIMAL?

The aye-aye (a nocturnal mammal from Madagascar) has one very long, bony finger on one hand. It looks so scary that people used to believe they would die if they came into contact with one.

WHY DOESN'T MY CAT ROAR?

Members of the cat family can either roar or purr—they can't do both. The ones that can roar are lions, jaguars, tigers, and leopards.

HOW LOUD IS A LION'S ROAR?

An adult lion's roar is so loud that it can be heard up to 8 km (5 miles) away.

HOW HIGH CAN BIG CATS JUMP?

Pumas and leopards are the highest jumpers of the big cat world— they can both reach a height of 5m (16.4 feet).

DID YOU KNOW?

Three-toed sloths often appear green. They move so slowly that algae grows on their fur!

HOW LONG DOES IT TAKE A SLOTH TO EAT ITS DINNER?

The contents of a sloth's stomach can take up to a month to be digested completely. That's a lot of rotten twigs and berries!

DO ANY ANIMALS HAVE THREE EYES?

The tuatara lizard of New Zealand has two normal eyes and a third placed neatly on the top of its head!

CAN A NEWT GROW NEW LEGS?

If they are injured or damaged, newts can regrow body parts, including legs, arms, and even a new heart!

HOW LONG WOULD IT TAKE TO FILL A SWIMMING POOL WITH MILK?

That depends on how many cows you have! It would take a year of milking 330 cows to gather the 2,575 metric tons (660,253 gallons) of the white stuff you would need to fill an Olympic-sized swimming pool.

DID YOU KNOW?

Cows can walk up steps but not down them.

ARE COWS DANGEROUS?

Being trampled by a cow is the cause of death for around 100 people each year.

ARE HIPPOS DANGEROUS?

Far more humans are killed by foul-tempered hippos than crocodiles or sharks. Hippos like to overturn boats, trample people, and even use their massive mouths to bite off heads.

DID YOU KNOW?

Early explorers thought that a giraffe was a cross between a camel and a leopard and called it cameleopard!

DO SQUIRRELS REMEMBER WHERE THEY BURY ALL THEIR NUTS?

Even though they spend most of the year hiding them for winter, most squirrels can't remember where they hide half of their nuts.

HOW LOUD IS A HOWLER MONKEY?

The call of the male howler monkey can be heard up to 16km (10 miles) away. That's twice as far as a lion's roar!

WHICH ANIMAL IS THE BRAINIEST?

In relation to body size, tree shrews have the largest brain of any animal.

DID YOU KNOW?

The collective name for a group of rhinoceros is a "crash." Very appropriate!

PECULIAR PETS

HOW MANY DIFFERENT SOUNDS CAN CATS AND DOGS MAKE?

Cats can make over 100 vocal sounds, while dogs can make only 10.

DID YOU KNOW?

A cat's brain is actually more similar to a human brain than that of a dog. Cats and humans have identical regions in the brain that are responsible for emotion.

WHO HAS THE BEST MEMORY—A CAT OR DOG?

Cats have better memories than dogs. Tests have concluded that a dog's short-term memory lasts no more than five minutes; a cat's can last as long as 16 hours.

HOW CAN YOU TELL WHO IS THE BOSS DOG?

When two male dogs approach each other, the dog that wags its tail the slowest is the dominant one.

105-3120A
Assault and Cattery

DID YOU KNOW?

Cat urine glows in the dark when ultraviolet light shines on it.

HAVE CATS EVER BEEN ARRESTED?

In 2006, Lewis the cat was put under house arrest by police in Connecticut, USA, because of his unprovoked attacks on local people. He was even placed in a line-up and picked out as the guilty party by a number of his victims.

DO HAMSTERS HAVE GOOD MEMORIES?

Hamsters can still recognize and remember their hamster relatives even if they have been separated for a long time.

DID YOU KNOW?

Baby hamsters are called "pups."

WHAT DO HAMSTERS EAT IN THE WILD?

In the wild, a hamster's winter food store can be huge. Some contain over 1.5 million seeds!

HOW FAR DOES A HAMSTER RUN ON A WHEEL?

On average, a hamster will run up to 9.6km (6 miles)
a night on an exercise wheel.

DID YOU KNOW?

Most hamsters blink with one eye at a time.

HOW DO HAMSTERS REMEMBER THEIR ROUTE HOME?

When in unfamiliar territory, a hamster will rub its scent
glands (found along its sides) against various objects.
This leaves a scent trail the hamster can follow to go
the other way!

HOW GOOD IS A DOG'S HEARING?

Experiments have shown that dogs can locate the source of a sound in 0.06 seconds by using their ears like rotating radar dishes.

DID YOU KNOW?

It is against the law for a dog to fly a kite on most public beaches in the USA.

HOW DO DOGS SWEAT?

Contrary to popular belief, dogs do not sweat by panting—they sweat through the pads of their feet. Panting is used to lower their overall body temperature.

ARE CANARIES FROM THE CANARY ISLANDS?

The Canary Islands were not named after the canary bird but after the large dogs that lived on the islands. In Latin, the name of the island group was Canariae Insulae, which translates as "Islands of the Dogs."

WHERE DOES THE WORD BUDGERIGAR COME FROM?

When European settlers asked the native Aboriginal Australians the name of the noisy native birds, the Aboriginals replied "betchery-gah." Only later did settlers discover that betcherygah—which became budgerigar—actually meant "good to eat"!

DID YOU KNOW?

A budgerigar by the name of Puck has the largest animal vocabulary, entering the Guinness Book of World Records in 1995 with a hefty 1,728 words.

CAN YOU TRAIN CATS TO DO JOBS?

37 cats were employed to carry bundles of letters to villages in Liège, Belgium, in 1879. The cats proved pretty undisciplined and the service didn't last long. Yet the creators seemed surprised at the failure!

DID YOU KNOW?

Every cat's noseprint is unique just like a human fingerprint.

HOW SENSITIVE ARE A CAT'S WHISKERS?

Cats' whiskers can detect movements 2,000 times smaller than the width of a human hair.

HOW MUCH FOOD DOES A CAT EAT IN A YEAR?

In a single year, the average cat consumes nearly 28 times its own weight in food and the same amount in liquids.

WHY IS CAT FOOD NOT MADE OF MICE?

Pet food manufacturers once developed a mousey cat food, but cats just didn't like the taste.

DID YOU KNOW?

Cats are unable to survive on a purely meat-free diet.

WHY CAN'T DOGS EAT CHOCOLATE?

Chocolate can be deadly to a dog's heart and nervous system. Just a handful of chocolate chips is enough to kill a small dog.

DO RABBITS EAT THEIR OWN POOP?

Rabbits partially digest the grass they eat and then excrete it as soft, gluey pellets. They then eat these pellets to finish digesting their meal. Yummy!

IS THERE A CURE FOR DOG POOP?

To solve the problem of dog poop left on city streets, Dutch scientists developed a dog food that is almost entirely absorbed by dogs, leaving only 10 percent waste. Dogs eating the new food produce only a small, dry pellet of poop.

WHY SHOULD FERRET OWNERS WATCH WHERE THEY SIT?

A large number of pet ferrets are squashed each year by reclining chairs. The ferret curls up under the chair and then gets squished when its unknowing owner puts the seat back up.

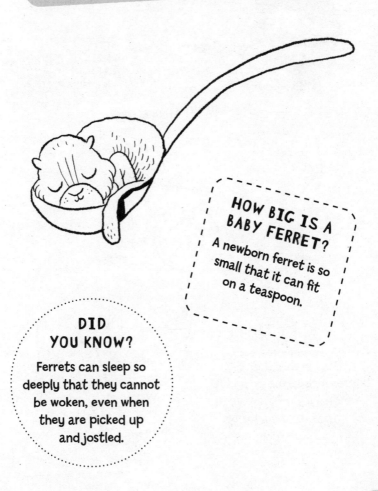

HOW BIG IS A BABY FERRET?

A newborn ferret is so small that it can fit on a teaspoon.

DID YOU KNOW?

Ferrets can sleep so deeply that they cannot be woken, even when they are picked up and jostled.

WHAT IS THE HEAVIEST-EVER DOG?

The heaviest dog on record is an old English mastiff named Zorba, who weighed 155kg (343lbs). That's the same as two adult male humans.

WHAT IS THE SMALLEST BREED OF CAT?

Weighing only 1.8kg (4lbs), the Singapura is the smallest breed of domestic cat. That's the same weight as a medium-sized pineapple.

DID YOU KNOW?

Dogs in New York City produce 18 million kg (40 million lbs) of poop every year. That's a lot of pooper-scoopers!

HOW MANY BABIES DO RABBITS HAVE?

The largest rabbit litter on record contained 24 babies. The average number of rabbits in a litter is about six!

WHAT DO YOU CALL A RABBIT'S TAIL?

The proper name for a rabbit's fluffy tail is a "scut."

DID YOU KNOW?

Because of the position of their eyes, rabbits can see behind them without turning their heads.

HAS A DOG EVEN BEEN INTO SPACE?

Laika the dog was the world's first astronaut. She was sent into space by the Russian government aboard a satellite in 1957.

ARE THERE ANY MICE ASTRONAUTS?

Three mice named Mia, Laska, and Benji were sent into space by NASA in 1958.

DID LAIKA SURVIVE?

Laika was also the world's first space casualty after dying from stress and overheating a few hours after take-off.

WHERE DOES THE SAYING "RAINING CATS AND DOGS" COME FROM?

During heavy downpours in 17th-century England, many stray cats and dogs would float down the narrow streets.

DID YOU KNOW?

The punishment for killing a greyhound in ancient Egypt was the same as for killing a human.

WHAT IS THE OLDEST BREED OF DOG?

The saluki is the oldest breed of domestic dog, dating back to ancient Mesopotamia (around 3000BC). Before this, all dogs were actually wild wolves.

DO PEOPLE PREFER THEIR PETS OVER HUMANS?

In a pet-insurance survey, more than 50 percent of pet owners said they would rather be stranded on a desert island with their pet than with another person.

HOW LONG DO GOLDFISH LIVE FOR?

A goldfish can live for over 40 years.

DID YOU KNOW?

Customs officials at Melbourne Airport, Australia, were suspicious when they heard splashing sounds coming from a woman's skirt. It turned out she was smuggling 51 live tropical fish in a water-filled apron!

CAN DOGS FLY?

A dog named Brutus became the world's highest-skydiving dog in 1997 after making a jump of 1,393m (4,572 ft).

DID YOU KNOW?

The bloodhound is the only animal whose evidence can be used in a US court.

HOW WELL DO RABBITS TASTE?

A rabbit's tongue contains 17,000 taste buds. That's over 7,000 more than an average human!

WHAT DO BABY BUNNIES SMELL LIKE?

Baby bunnies have no smell at all, which helps protect them from predators.

HOW LONG CAN RABBITS LIVE?

The longest-living rabbit on record was nearly 19 years old when he died.

CAN CATS SEE IN THE DARK?

A cat has a layer of extra cells in its eyes that absorb light, allowing it to see six times better at night than a human.

DID YOU KNOW?

A cat's jaw cannot move sideways.

ARE CATS LAZY?

Cats are among the laziest animals, sleeping up to 18 hours a day. Cats fall asleep quickly but wake up frequently to check that their environment is safe from predators. That's where the term "cat nap" comes from, meaning a short snooze.

DO PEOPLE EAT GUINEA PIGS?

Guinea pig meat is always on the menu in Peru and Bolivia where the animals are bred as food.

DID YOU KNOW?

The Latin name for a gerbil, meriones unguiculatus, means "clawed warrior."

ARE THERE ANY DOG MILLIONAIRES?

The USA is home to some very pampered pooches, with an estimated 1 million dogs having been named as the main beneficiary in their owners' wills! When Ella Wendel from New York died in 1931 she left a sizeable fortune of US$30 million/£22,464,000 to her beloved Toby—her pet poodle!

HOW WELL DO DOGS SMELL?

A dog's sense of smell is one of the most advanced in the world. If a stew was cooking, a human would smell the overall aroma, whereas a dog would smell all of the ingredients individually. A dog has up to 150 square cm (23 square inches) of olfactory membrane—the area in the brain used to detect smells. A human has just 4 square cm (0.62 square inches).

WHAT ABOUT CATS?

A cat can't smell as well as a dog, but its sense of smell is 14 times stronger than a human's.

DID YOU KNOW?

Cats do not like the smell of oranges and lemons.

HOW MANY MICE CAN A CAT CATCH?

The largest number of mice caught by a single cat is 28,899 over a 24-year period. That's about four mice a day, every day!

IS EATING MICE GOOD FOR CATS?

A cat would have to eat five mice to gain the same nutritional value as the average canned or dry cat food.

DID YOU KNOW?

Every year, people in the USA spend 62 percent more on pet food than on baby food.

DO DOGS HAVE FACIAL EXPRESSIONS?

Dogs have about 100 different facial expressions, most of them made using their ears. Unfortunately, bulldogs and pit bull terriers only have about 10.

CAN DOGS ANSWER THE PHONE?

Around 30 percent of US pet owners admit to talking to their dogs or leaving messages on their answering machines for their dogs while they are away.

DID YOU KNOW?

A Pekingese dog belonging to Henry Sleeper Harper and a Pomeranian dog belonging to Miss Margaret Hays are listed among the survivors of the Titanic.

WHY DO CATS KEEP GROOMING THEMSELVES?

Cats always clean themselves after they eat to remove any food smells that predators could notice and want to investigate!

WHAT IS THE HEAVIEST-EVER CAT?

The heaviest cat on record was Himmy, an Australian cat, who weighed 21.3kg (46.8lbs). No other cat has weighed so much since!

DID YOU KNOW?

A cat's heart beats twice as fast as a human's.

CAN DOGS SURVIVE COLD TEMPERATURES?

Siberian Huskies can live and work in temperatures as low as -60 °C (-75 °F).

WHAT DOES THE NAME "DACHSHUND" MEAN?

Dachshund means "badger dog"—the dogs were originally bred for digging badgers out from their setts.

DID YOU KNOW?

Poodles were originally used in Europe as hunting dogs. Imagine!

HOW MUCH DOES IT COST TO LOOK AFTER A DOG?

Based on an average life span of 11 years, the cost of owning a dog is US$13,350 or £9,991.

ARE SOME PEOPLE AFRAID OF CATS?

Ailurophobia is a fear of cats. Julius Caesar, Henry II, Charles XI, and Napoleon were all sufferers and would nearly faint in the presence of a cat.

DID YOU KNOW?

Approximately seven percent of cats and 21 percent of dogs snore.

FEATHERED FACTS

HOW STRONG ARE BALD EAGLES?

Bald eagles can fly carrying 2–3kg (4–7lbs) of food in their talons. Try carrying four bags of sugar to see how heavy it is!

IS A BALD EAGLE REALLY BALD?

Not really. It actually has white feathers on its head, neck, and tail. The "bald" part comes from the Old English word balde, meaning "white."

CAN EAGLES SWIM?

Bald eagles can swim! They use an overhand movement of their wings that is similar to the butterfly stroke.

ARE THERE BIRDS THAT FEED ON BLOOD?

The vampire finch is so called because of its habit of pecking other birds and feeding on their blood!

CAN BIRDS GET TOO FULL TO FLY?

Vultures sometimes eat so much that they become too heavy to fly. They have to vomit to bring their weight down.

ARE ANY BIRDS POISONOUS?

Pitohui birds eat a certain type of beetle that makes their skin and feathers poisonous to predators.

WHY DO HUMMINGBIRDS EAT SO OFTEN?

If humans had the same metabolism (digestion rate) as hummingbirds, we would have to eat about 155,000 calories a day to stay alive—that's about 77 times the normal amount!

CAN HUMMINGBIRDS WALK?

No. A hummingbird's legs are so light and flimsy that it can't walk; it can only perch or fly.

DID YOU KNOW?

The hummingbird is the only bird that can fly backward.

HOW SMALL ARE HUMMINGBIRD EGGS?

Hummingbird eggs are so small that your thumbnail would completely cover three of them.

HOW DOES A TURKEY VULTURE KEEP COOL?

The turkey vulture covers its legs in poop to keep cool when it is hot.

DO BIRDS PLAY FOOTBALL?

Turkeys and chickens like to play with objects and toss them around. No word on the first chicken football team yet, though!

DID YOU KNOW?

American turkey vultures help humans detect broken underground fuel pipes. The leaking fuel smells like carrion (the dead animals they eat). The clusters of birds standing around leaks show the engineers where repairs are needed.

CAN PENGUINS FLY?

Penguins can jump nearly 3m (10ft) into the air ... but they can't fly!

DID YOU KNOW?

Penguin urine accounts for nearly three percent of the ice in Antarctic glaciers.

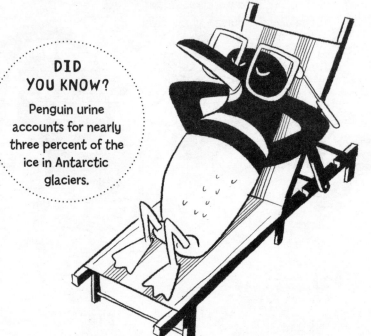

DO ALL PENGUINS LIVE AT THE SOUTH POLE?

Not all penguins live in cold climates—the Galápagos penguin lives near the Equator in temperatures of up to 29°C/ 84°F.

HOW DEEP DO PENGUINS DIVE?

The emperor penguin regularly dives to depths of 550m (1,800ft). The world record for the deepest human scuba dive is 332m (1,090ft).

HOW LONG CAN A PENGUIN GO WITHOUT FOOD?

A male emperor penguin will go without food for up to 115 days while incubating the eggs laid by its female partner.

DID YOU KNOW?

During deep-sea dives, gentoo penguins reduce their heart rate from around 100 to just 20 beats per minute.

CAN BABY BIRDS CLIMB TREES?

Hoatzin chicks from South America can. They use special claws to move around until their wings are strong enough for them to fly.

DID YOU KNOW?

Birds that lay their eggs in the nests of other birds often check to see if their eggs are being cared for. If they have been removed, the birds vandalize the nest, killing any other eggs or chicks.

HOW MANY WORMS DOES A CHICK EAT?

If you laid end to end all the earthworms eaten by a baby robin in one day, they would stretch to 4m (13ft).

WHY DO OWLS TURN THEIR HEADS?

Some owls can turn their heads round at a 270-degree angle. They have to do this because their eyes are too large to move in their eye sockets.

DID YOU KNOW?

The burrowing owl of North and South America makes its nest underground and lines it with cow dung for warmth.

WHAT IS AN OWL PELLET?

Owls swallow their prey (mostly mice and voles) whole. The parts they cannot digest, like fur and bones, are formed into small pellets that the owl vomits up.

WHICH BIRDS HAVE THE MOST AND LEAST FEATHERS?

The whistling swan has the most feathers of any bird, with over 25,000. The bird with the lowest number of feathers is the ruby-throated hummingbird. It only has 940 of them!

DID YOU KNOW?

The feathers of a pigeon weigh more than its bones!

HOW LONG CAN FEATHERS GROW?

The phoenix fowl of Japan boasts the longest tail feathers of any bird, with some having tails that stretch to 10m (34 ft).

WHY DO DUCKS SLEEP IN GROUPS?

Ducks gather in groups to sleep. Those on the outer edge sleep with one eye open to watch for predators.

WHY DON'T DUCKS GET FROZEN FEET IN WINTER?

Ducks' feet contain no nerves or blood vessels. This means they never feel the cold when they swim in icy water.

HOW DO HOODED MERGANSER DUCKLINGS STAY SAFE?

Hooded merganser ducklings from Canada gather together when in the water and form a tight compact group to protect them from predators. To hawks flying above them, they look just like a large swimming rodent.

WHAT IS THE WORLD'S MOST COMMON BIRD?

The chicken is the most common bird on the planet, with over 24 billion of them worldwide.

CAN CHICKENS FLY?

The longest recorded flight for a chicken is 13 seconds.

DID YOU KNOW?

In the 19th century, people sometimes cleaned their chimneys by dropping live chickens down them. The chickens would dislodge soot by beating their wings inside.

HOW DO YOU HYPNOTIZE A CHICKEN?

You can hypnotize a chicken by repeatedly drawing a line on the ground in front of it. The chicken will stay in the same spot as long as you keep drawing the line!

DID YOU KNOW?

If a chicken has red wattles (the floppy pieces that hang down from their necks and heads), it will only produce brown eggs. If it has white wattles, it will only produce white eggs.

CAN YOU GET MORE THAN ONE YOLK IN A CHICKEN EGG?

Occasionally a chicken egg will produce two or more yolks. The most ever found in a single egg is nine! Sometimes a chicken egg can contain another complete egg inside it. This happens when an egg goes back up into a chicken, meets another egg on the way down and the second egg forms around the first one!

HOW MANY WORDS CAN A PARROT LEARN?

If you fancy a chat, have a look for an African gray (or grey) parrot—it has vocabulary of over 800 words!

DID YOU KNOW?

Alex the African gray parrot at Brandeis University, Massachusetts, USA, was taught to learn shapes, shades, and materials, and had the communication skills of a two-year-old child. He could even tell lab assistants what he wanted them to change in his living environment!

HOW LONG DO PARROTS LIVE?

Larger parrots, such as macaws and cockatoos, can live for more than 75 years.

CAN BIRDS GET SEASICK?

Yes. If you keep an albatross on a boat, it can get seasick.

HOW DO PETRELS KEEP HUMANS AWAY?

The southern giant petrel likes to vomit smelly stomach oils and regurgitated food at predators or nosy humans.

CAN BIRDS SLEEP IN THE AIR?

The sooty tern only lands to breed and rear its young. It eats, sleeps, and drinks while flying and can stay airborne for 10 years! An albatross also sleeps while it flies! It can doze while cruising at 40km/h (25mph).

WHICH BIRDS FLY THE FURTHEST?

The Arctic tern flies a round trip of 35,000km (21,750 miles) a year, breeding in the Arctic in the northern summer and feeding in the Antarctic during the southern summer. The bar-tailed godwit migrates farther in a single trip than any other bird. Each year it travels non-stop from Alaska to New Zealand in just nine days and loses over half of its body weight on the trip.

DO BIRDS WEAR SUNGLASSES?

Some sea birds, such as gulls and terns, have red oil in their eyes. This acts like a pair of sunglasses that protect their eyes from the glare of bright sunlight.

WHICH BIRD HAS THE LONGEST WINGS?

The largest wingspan ever recorded for a living bird was 3.63m (11.9ft) for a wandering albatross, caught in 1965.

WHICH BIRD IS THE STUPIDEST?

The brain of an ostrich is very small compared to its body size, making it one of the stupidest birds around.

HOW LONG DOES IT TAKE TO COOK AN OSTRICH EGG?

It takes 40 minutes to hard-boil an ostrich egg.

DID YOU KNOW?

To get at the tasty insides of hard-shelled ostrich eggs, the Egyptian vulture drops stones on them from the air to crack them open.

DO SWANS HAVE **THEIR** OWN SONG?

The term "swan song" comes from the ancient Greeks, who believed that a swan sang a song of death when its life was about to end.

WHO OWNS ENGLAND'S SWANS?

All wild swans in England are the property of the Queen, who has an official swan keeper.

DID YOU KNOW?

When police raided an elderly Swedish woman's apartment in 2007 they found that she had been sheltering 11 swans for more than five years!

HOW SHARP IS A FALCON'S EYESIGHT?

A falcon can spot an object the size of a mouse from nearly 3km (2 miles) away.

HOW FAST CAN A FALCON FLY?

A peregrine falcon can fly speeds of 320km/h (200mph) when diving through the air to catch its prey.

DID YOU KNOW?

New York City is home to the world's largest urban population of peregrine falcons.

WHICH BIRD EATS WITH ITS HEAD UPSIDE DOWN?

Because of the design of its beak, a flamingo always eats with its head upside down.

WHY IS A FLAMINGO PINK?

A flamingo is pink because of the shrimp that it eats. A flamingo that doesn't eat shrimp will be almost white!

DID YOU KNOW?

The ancient Romans used to eat the rather stomach-churning delicacy of flamingo tongues.

WHAT IS A TOUCAN'S BEAK MADE OF?

A toucan's beak is made of keratin, the same stuff from which your hair and nails are made.

WHICH BIRD IS THE BEST MIMIC?

Australian lyrebirds can perfectly imitate hundreds of sounds, including car alarms, chainsaws, and even the clicking of tourists' cameras—learned from being photographed in the wild!

CAN BIRDS SWEAT?

No. Up to three quarters of the air a bird breathes is used for cooling down its body.

HOW HIGH CAN BIRDS FLY?

Geese have been found flying at heights of up to 8km (5 miles) above the ground. A jumbo jet cruises at around 12km (7.5 miles)!

WHY DON'T WOODPECKERS GET HEADACHES?

Woodpeckers slam their heads into trees at a rate of 20 pecks per second. A spongy area behind their beaks acts as a shock absorber and stops them from getting a headache.

HOW DID THE BUTCHER BIRD GET ITS NAME?

The shrike got its nickname of "butcher bird" from its habit of impaling its prey on spikes to hold it still while devouring it.

DID YOU KNOW?

The longest name of any bird is Griseotyrannus aurantioatrocristatus, otherwise known as the Crowned Slaty Flycatcher of South America.

HOW DID THE TAILORBIRD GET ITS NAME?

The tailorbird punches holes in leaves with its sharp bill and uses long grass to stitch them together to make a nest.

IS THERE A BIRD LIKE A VELOCIRAPTOR?

Yes. The cassowary bird of New Guinea and Australia has a dagger-like, 12cm (5 inch)-long, razor-sharp claw that can disembowel an enemy with a single kick.

DID YOU KNOW?

Only male canaries can sing.

DO BIRDS USE BAIT?

Green herons have been known to drop berries, insects, and other objects onto the surface of the water to attract fish. When a nosy fish comes to investigate, the heron strikes and bags himself a tasty snack.

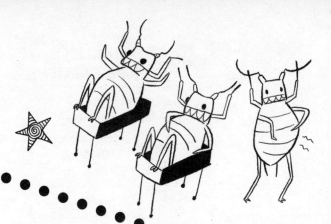

CREEPY CRAWLIES

HOW MANY INSECTS ARE THERE ON EARTH?

There are around 1.4 billion insects for every one human on Earth.

HOW MUCH DO ALL THE WORLD'S INSECTS EAT?

Insects eat 10 percent of the world's food supply each year. You'll never catch them pushing a shopping cart around the supermarket, though!

HOW DO YOU TURN A COCKROACH INTO A ZOMBIE?

The female jewel wasp can turn a cockroach into a "zombie" by stinging it in the head. The cockroach lies paralyzed while the wasp lays its eggs in its body, dying only when the hatched wasp larva chews its way out of the cockroach's stomach.

DID YOU KNOW?

Wasps that feed on fermented fruit occasionally get drunk and pass out.

IS A TARANTULA HAWK A SPIDER OR A BIRD?

Neither! The tarantula hawk is actually a wasp. The female wasp attacks and paralyzes a tarantula spider before laying an egg in its body. The hatched wasp then eats the tarantula alive as its first meal.

DO FEMALE SPIDERS EAT MALES?

The female black widow spider eats the male after mating, sometimes eating up to 25 partners a day. Now that's a real man-eater!

DID YOU KNOW?

Tarantula spiders cannot spin webs.

HOW DO SPIDERS EAT?

When it's time for dinner, a spider traps its prey before injecting it with a chemical that turns the bug's insides to mush. The spider then sucks out the liquid like a bug milkshake.

WHAT IS THE WORLD'S HEAVIEST SPIDER?

The record for the world's heaviest spider was a giant bird-eating spider found in Suriname in 1965. It weighed 122g (4 ounces). That's about the same as a large apple!

DID YOU KNOW?

There are 35,000 species of spider but only 27 are known to be deadly to humans.

CAN HUMANS USE SPIDER WEBS?

Eastern European peasants used to make wound dressings out of spiders' webs. Spider silk has antiseptic properties, so it wasn't such a bad idea.

WHY CAN'T YOU FEEL A LEECH BITE?

You can't feel the bite of a leech because it produces a natural painkiller before latching on. How thoughtful!

HOW MUCH BLOOD DOES A LEECH DRINK?

A leech will only finish sucking blood when it is five times its original size. The blood consumed in a single meal can keep a leech alive for up to nine months.

DID YOU KNOW?

A leech has 32 brains. Some leeches have 300 teeth, with 100 in each of their three bloodsucking jaws.

HOW MUCH DO CATERPILLARS EAT?

The caterpillar of the polyphemus moth chomps its way through 86,000 times its own birth weight in food in the first 56 days of its life. That would be the same as a human baby munching through about 150,000 burgers!

ARE ANY CATERPILLARS POISONOUS?

The guts of the African n'gwa caterpillar are so poisonous that hunters could use them to tip their spears and arrowheads.

DID YOU KNOW?

Greenfly, or aphids, are actually born pregnant with clones (exact copies of themselves) that they later give birth to. Weird!

CAN ANTS EAT HUGE ANIMALS?

Fearsome driver ants move in such massive colonies that they can strip the flesh from any animal down to the bone. They have been known to completely devour wounded lions and crocodiles.

DID YOU KNOW?

The Australian bulldog ant can kill a human in 15 minutes by clinging onto a person's skin with its strong jaws and stinging over and over again.

HOW MUCH CAN ANTS CARRY?

Ants can carry a load about 100 times their own body weight.

WHAT WEIGHS MORE—ALL THE ANTS IN THE WORLD, OR ALL THE PEOPLE?

2,000 years ago, the total weight of the world's ants would have been more than the total weight of the world's humans. Now, though, humans weigh more.

HOW DO WEAVER ANTS BUILD THEIR NESTS?

To build their nests, weaver ants line up in a row and use their mandibles (jaws) to pull nearby leaves together. They then squeeze their larvae so that they produce a fine thread of silk, which is used to "stitch" the nest together.

DID YOU KNOW?

Ants, termites, grasshoppers, and wasps were all around during the time of the dinosaurs.

WHAT'S THE BIGGEST COCKROACH IN THE WORLD?

The largest cockroaches in the world are the colossus cockroaches of Columbia. They can grow bigger than the palm of your hand.

CAN COCKROACHES SURVIVE EXTREME COLD?

A cockroach can survive being frozen in a block of ice for two days.

CAN COCKROACHES SURVIVE UNDERWATER?

A cockroach can hold its breath underwater for up to 40 minutes.

CAN COCKROACHES SURVIVE WITHOUT THEIR HEAD?

A cockroach can live for a week after having its head cut off. It only dies from starvation.

HOW FAST DO COCKROACHES BREED?

Cockroaches breed so fast that if a single pair reproduced for a year, with all their babies reproducing as well, there would be ten million of them altogether.

DO COCKROACHES MAKE A NOISE?

A cockroach can "hiss" by squeezing air out of tiny holes in its body. It can be heard up to 3.5m (11ft) away.

DID YOU KNOW?

In order to crawl into tiny cracks, cockroaches can flatten their bodies to just a little thicker than a piece of paper.

WHAT IS A SNAIL'S SLIME FOR?

Protection! The slime produced by snails is so protectively slimy that a snail could crawl along the edge of a razor blade without cutting itself.

ARE THERE ANY DANGEROUS SNAILS?

Yes, absolutely. The sting of a tropical cone snail can be fatal to a human being. Luckily, they live underwater, so you should be safe in your garden.

HOW BIG CAN SNAILS GROW?

The giant African land snail can grow to 39cm (15 inches) and weigh 900g (2lbs).

WHICH SCORPION IS THE DEADLIEST TO HUMANS?

The fat-tailed scorpion is responsible for most human deaths from scorpion stings. Although its venom is less toxic than that of the deathstalker scorpion, it injects more into its victim.

DID YOU KNOW?

A scorpion can withstand up to 200 times the amount of radiation that would kill a human.

DO ALL MOSQUITOES SUCK BLOOD?

Only female mosquitos drink human blood. They do it to get the protein they need to lay eggs. A mosquito can drink one and a half times its own weight in blood in a single meal.

WHY ARE MOSQUITO BITES ITCHY?

When a mosquito bites you, the enzymes in its saliva cause you to itch, not the bite itself.

DID YOU KNOW?

Mosquitoes are strongly attracted to people who have recently eaten bananas.

HOW MANY MOSQUITOES HATCH IN THE SUMMER?

The number of mosquitoes that hatch during the Arctic summer is so great that their swarms blot out the Sun.

DID YOU KNOW?

A patch of rainforest soil almost the size of this book can contain 10,000 mosquito eggs.

CAN WORMS SURVIVE BEING CUT IN HALF?

If cut in half in the right place, a healthy earthworm can grow a new head or tail. Of course, the worm might think there is no "right place" to be cut in half!

HOW DO WORMS TASTE?

An earthworm tastes with its whole body—it has taste receptors spread all over it. Every time you pick one up, they get a little taste of you, too!

DID YOU KNOW?

Earthworms have five hearts! They help them breathe, as the veins closest to the skin take in oxygen.

ARE THERE MANY WORMS IN THE WORLD?

Yes! 80 percent of all animals are nematode worms—simple worms found everywhere, including salt and fresh water, soil, and inside plants and animals.

HOW LONG CAN WORMS GROW?

The Giant Gippsland Earthworm of Australia can grow up to 3m (10ft) in length. That's almost as long as a python.

DID YOU KNOW?

If you weighed all of the people who live in the USA, and all of the earthworms in the USA, the earthworms would weigh 50 times more!

HOW CAN A CRICKET TELL YOU THE TEMPERATURE?

You can find out the temperature outside (in degrees Fahrenheit) by counting a cricket's chirps for 14 seconds and adding 40.

DID YOU KNOW?

To help transport their communication sounds, some crickets burrow tunnels in the earth, which act as megaphones. The sound can be heard from 610m (2,000ft) away.

HOW MANY LOCUSTS MIGHT YOU FIND IN A SWARM?

Locusts travel in swarms of up to 80 million. Between 20-30 July 1874, a swarm of Rock Mountain locusts flew over Nebraska, covering an area approximately 515,000 square km (198,840 square miles).

HOW FAR DOES A BEE FLY TO COLLECT NECTAR FOR HONEY?

A honeybee travels an average of 1,60 round trips in order to produce six teaspoons of honey. To produce 1kg (2.2lbs) of honey, a bee has to travel a distance equal to four times around the Earth.

HOW MANY BEES LIVE IN A BEEHIVE?

There are approximately 40-45,000 bees in an average beehive. Remember that next time you go looking for honey!

DID YOU KNOW?

Africanized bees have been known to pursue an enemy for more than 0.5. km (0.25 miles). Never upset an Africanized bee unless you have a very fast car!

HOW MANY DIFFERENT BEETLES ARE THERE?

There are at least 3,700 species of beetle in Britain alone. Just hope they don't all pop around for a visit at once!

DID YOU KNOW?

The American burying beetle uses the fur of dead animals to build its nest.

WHAT IS THE BIGGEST BEETLE?

The Goliath beetle is the world's biggest bug, weighing in at 99g (3.5 ounces) during their larval stage, and is 11.5cm (4.5 inches) long.

HOW BRIGHT IS THE LIGHT OF A FIREFLY?

Fireflies are not really flies—they are a type of beetle. The light from six large fireflies is enough to read by. Pretty handy on a summer's evening!

HOW MANY BUGS COULD YOU FIND IN ONE SQUARE MILE?

In just 2.5 square km (1 square mile) of rural land, you could find more insects than there are humans on the entire planet!

DID YOU KNOW?

A dragonfly has two sets of wings that can flap independently of each other. Their front wings can be going up while their back ones are going down!

HOW BIG ARE BIRD-EATING SPIDERS?

Goliath bird-eating spiders are so huge that they can grow to the size of a dinner plate. The largest known example was found in Venezuela in 1965 and measured 28cm (11 inches) across. That's almost as long as your school ruler!

DID YOU KNOW?

Female tarantulas can live for up to 30 years.

ARE CRANEFLIES DANGEROUS?

No. Despite the popular myth, a cranefly's legs' venom is not dangerous to humans. It has never been studied in depth as the poor arachnid cannot open its jaws wide enough to be able to bite humans.

WHY IS IT HARD TO SWAT A FLY?

A fly can react to something it sees and change its flying direction in just 30 thousandths of a second.

DO FLIES REALLY TASTE WITH THEIR FEET?

Flies can taste what they are standing on because of the 1,500 tiny taste hairs on their feet. A housefly's feet are 10 million times more sensitive to sugar than a human tongue is.

DID YOU KNOW?

To land on your ceiling, a fly has to grab hold with its front legs and then do a somersault in order to bring its back legs into contact with the ceiling.

DO TERMITES EXPLODE?

To defend their territory, guard termites sometimes make themselves explode to scare off attackers.

HOW MANY EGGS DOES A QUEEN TERMITE LAY?

Queen termites lay an egg every second for up to 10 years.

CAN A QUEEN TERMITE REALLY LIVE FOR 50 YEARS?

Yes. The poor workers that keep her well looked after only live for one or two years!

HOW HIGH AND FAST CAN A FLEA JUMP?

The jumping ability of a flea is the equivalent of an adult human jumping over a 25-floor building. Relative to their size, fleas can accelerate 50 times faster than the space shuttle!

HOW STRONG IS A SPIDER'S SILK?

Spiders' silk is stronger than steel. If you stretched equalized threads of steel and spiders' silk, the steel thread would break first.

DID YOU KNOW?

If two flies were left to reproduce for a year, without threat from predators, the resulting mass of flies would be the size of planet Earth!

DO MOTHS EAT CLOTHES?

A clothing moth's preferred meal is a dirty woolly sweater. The more sweat, food, and oils there are, the better.

DID YOU KNOW?

Instead of giving birth, a pregnant scorpion can sometimes reabsorb its babies back into its body.

HOW LONG DO SNAILS SLEEP FOR?

Snails can sleep for up to three years in one single snooze.

SLIMY STUFF

WHAT DO MALE VULTURES DO TO ATTRACT FEMALES?

Female Egyptian vultures are attracted to the male with the yellowest face. Unfortunately for the males, they have to eat their own poop to achieve this look!

HOW DOES A HORNED LIZARD DEFEND ITSELF?

The horned lizard from the southwestern US and Mexico can shoot blood out of its eyes when under attack.

DID YOU KNOW?

Cows only partly digest the grass they eat—after swallowing, they vomit it back up into their mouths, chew it, then swallow it again.

DO AMPHIBIAN BABIES EAT THEIR OWN MOTHERS?

The babies of the Boulengerula taitanus (a worm-like amphibian) actually eat their own mother's skin. The babies use special teeth when born to squirm all over their mother's body and remove her flesh. Somehow the mother usually survives!

HOW BIG IS THE BIGGEST ANT COLONY?

The world's largest ant colony was discovered in 2002. The interconnecting nests stretch 5,760km (3,579 miles) from the Italian Riviera into northern Spain. The super colony is home to several billion ants.

DID YOU KNOW?

A frog juice market stall in Lima, Peru, offers visitors a refreshing drink of skinned frogs blended into a smoothie. The locals claim this tasty treat cures a range of illnesses.

WHAT IS KANGAROO POOP USED FOR?

In Tasmania, kangaroo manure has been used to make environmentally friendly paper.

HOW LONG IS A WOODPECKER TONGUE?

A woodpecker's tongue can be as long as its body! It has a barb on the end of it for skewering grubs.

DID YOU KNOW?

Roger Dier of Petaluna, California, USA, kept 1,000 rats. Not too bad until you realize he kept them all in his one-bedroom home!

HOW DOES THE TONGUE LOUSE FIND FOOD?

The tongue louse is a type of parasite that crawls in through a fish's gills and then chews off the fish's tongue. It spends the rest of its life acting as its victim's tongue while feeding off the blood supply of the fish.

WHAT DOES A FACE FLY FEED ON?

The face fly feeds on the mucus produced in a cow's eyes and nostrils.

DID YOU KNOW?

A duckbilled platypus can stuff its cheek pouches with 600 worms at once.

HOW CAN RATS BE LESS SCARED OF CATS?

Toxoplasma gondii is a parasite that lives in rats' brains, changing their brains to make them less scared of cats. This means the rats are more likely to be caught and eaten, helping the parasite move easily into cats' brains—their preferred home.

DID YOU KNOW?

A scatologist is a person who studies animal poop.

HOW MUCH DO DOGS PEE IN PARKS?

Every year 4.5 million L (over 1 million gallons) of dog urine goes into the parks of London.

WHAT IS THE WORLD'S SMELLIEST ANIMAL?

The African zorilla (a type of polecat) could be the smelliest creature on the planet. The stench secreted from its anal glands can be detected up to 1km (half a mile) away.

CAN YOU SEE THROUGH A FROG?

Japanese scientists have bred completely see-through frogs so they can investigate their internal organs without having to kill and dissect them.

DID YOU KNOW?

The first recorded occurrence of a frog being sick was when one was taken on a space flight.

WHY DO HONEYBEES VIBRATE?

Honeybees will surround any intruder in their colony and vibrate. The vibrations create so much heat that the invader is literally cooked to death.

HOW MUCH DO COWS DROOL?

Cows produce 200 times more saliva than humans. Never ask a cow to blow out the candles on your birthday cake!

DID YOU KNOW?

A ribbon worm (a sea creature) can eat 95 percent of its own body—and still survive!

DO PEOPLE WORSHIP RATS?

A Hindu temple dedicated to the rat goddess Karni Mata in Deshnoke, India, houses more than 20,000 rats.

WHAT STRANGE THINGS DO PORCUPINES EAT?

Porcupines looking for salt have been known to eat tool handles and clothes because of the salty human sweat on them.

DID YOU KNOW?

The Argentinian wide-mouthed frog will eat prey as large as itself, sometimes eating to the point of ripping open its stomach.

CAN YOU EAT TERMITES?

In South Africa, termites are roasted and eaten as snacks, just like popcorn.

DO BABY BIRDS POOP IN THEIR NEST?

Yes. The great tit produces its feces in tiny sacs that it later removes from its nest. The average tit removes around 500 of these sacs from its nest each week—that's one busy little pooper!

DID YOU KNOW?

The highly prized Malaysian liqueur habu sake is made from fermented viper venom.

ARE SQUIRRELS DANGEROUS?

A pine-cone shortage in eastern Russia drove a gang of ravenous squirrels to attack and eat a stray dog.

DID YOU KNOW?

British artist Damien Hirst pickled a 4m (14ft) shark in formaldehyde. He called his work "The Physical Impossibility of Death in the Mind of Someone Living." The artwork was sold in 2004 for US$12 million/£9,018,000.

WHY WOULD YOU SPREAD COW DUNG ON YOUR WALLS?

Cow dung sets hard in hot countries and contains a natural mosquito repellent. Because of this, it is sometimes used to line floors and walls in buildings.

DID YOU KNOW?

Birds do not urinate—their urine and feces are all mixed together to make one sloppy dropping.

HOW MUCH DOES A BLACK RHINO POOP?

The African black rhinoceros excretes its own weight in dung every 48 hours. That's 682kg (1,500lbs) a day.

WHY DID THE POLAR BEAR TURN GREEN?

In 2004, the polar bears in Singapore Zoo turned green! The change from white was due to a type of algae growing in their hollow hair shafts.

DID YOU KNOW?

The female tahr (a relative of the goat) from India lets the male know she is ready for mating by urinating on him. Nice!

WHICH ANIMALS HAVE BLUE TONGUES?

Four animals have blue tongues— the black bear, the chow chow dog, the giraffe, and the blue-tongued skink.

CAN WHALES EXPLODE?

A decomposing sperm whale exploded in Taiwan in 2004 as it was being transported for a post mortem. Nearby shops and cars were showered with blood, guts, and blubber. A build-up of natural gases inside the whale was to blame.

DID YOU KNOW?

If it cannot find enough food, a baby Komodo dragon will eat its own brothers and sisters.

HOW LONG CAN TAPEWORMS GROW?

The biggest tapeworm ever found inside a human body was 35m (115ft) long.

DOES ANY CREATURE EAT HAIR?

The giant cricket of Africa enjoys eating human hair. Nobody knows why!

DID YOU KNOW?

British performance artist Paul Hurley wrapped himself in plastic wrap and wriggled about in a soggy field nibbling soil for nine days in 2004. He called his performance "Becoming Earthworm."

HOW FAR CAN STINKBUGS SPIT?

Some stinkbugs are able to spit their smelly goo as far as 30cm (1ft). Not bad for a bug often no more than 1.5cm (half an inch) long!

WHY SHOULD YOU NEVER DRINK A LEECH?

If you drink water with a leech in it, the tiny bloodsucker can attach to the inside of your mouth or throat and suck you dry from the inside.

DID YOU KNOW?

A crocodile's digestive juices contain so much hydrochloric acid that they have been found to dissolve everything from iron spearheads to six-inch steel hooks.

WHAT IS SPERMACETI?

The head of a sperm whale contains up to three tons of a substance called spermaceti. It turns hard and waxy while the whale is diving in the cold depths and becomes oilier and more liquid as the whale gets warmer. The oil used to be an ingredient in some types of makeup.

WHAT GROSS PLACE DO PEARLFISH LIVE IN?

The pearl ish swims into a sea cucumber's anus and lives inside it during the daytime, coming out only at night. The sea cucumber breathes through its anus, so it can't keep the fish out!

DID YOU KNOW?

Mammal blood is red, lobster blood is blue, and insect blood is yellow.

WHAT IS A WORM CAST?

The curly heaps of earth you find on the ground outside are called worm casts. They are actually little piles of worm poop.

HOW DO YOU CURE A POLAR BEAR'S BAD BREATH?

Vets at Seneca Park Zoo, USA, had to use a hammer and chisel to remove an infected tooth from a polar bear in 2005. The tooth had been giving the bear bad breath. How they got close enough to find out is a mystery!

DID YOU KNOW?

When a shark dies, it sinks so slowly to the bottom of the ocean that the salt water almost completely dissolves its corpse. The only parts that don't dissolve or get eaten are its teeth.

HOW DOES A HIPPO MARK ITS TERRITORY?

To mark its territory, a hippopotamus spins its tail while pooping, as the spinning helps spread the stinky stuff around.

WHAT'S IN BIRD'S NEST SOUP?

Cave swiftlets of Southeast Asia make nests from their own saliva. Locals use the dried nests to make the delicacy bird's nest soup—yes, it's a soup made from spit!

HOW BIG IS A SINGLE ELEPHANT POO?

An elephant can produce a 38kg (83lb) pile of poop in one go. An elephant produces around 150kg (330lbs) of dung every day.

DID YOU KNOW?

Romanian health officials were called to the apartment of 74-year-old Gyenge Lajos after he complained about a gas-like smell. The cause was soon discovered—a dead cow in the man's apartment that had been a gift from a friend. The carcass had started to rot, yet he was still cutting pieces from it to eat.

WHICH AMAZON FISH IS SCARIER THAN A PIRANHA?

The candiru (an eel-like fish) lives in the Amazon River and is more feared than the piranha. The transparent fish can smell pee in the water and heads straight for the source. It enters the body of its victim and burrows toward a major blood vessel to feed.

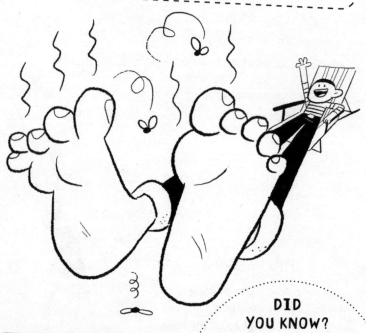

WHAT CREATURE LIKES SMELLY FEET?

Mosquitoes love stinky human feet because of the enzymes found on them.

DID YOU KNOW?

A mummified dog was found inside a tree 6m (20ft) above the ground in Georgia, USA. The hollow tree was the perfect condition to keep the dog preserved for 20 years after its death.

WHICH ANIMAL HAS ATTRACTIVE FARTS?

The fart of a female southern pine beetle contains a pheromone called frontalin, which attracts male beetles.

WHICH ANIMAL PEES AND EATS AT THE SAME TIME?

Vampire bats urinate the whole time that they're sucking blood. This ensures they don't get so full of blood that they're too heavy to fly.

DID YOU KNOW?

When a toad is sick, it vomits up its entire stomach. It hangs out of its mouth for a short time before being swallowed back down.

WHICH ANIMAL HAS A TOUGH BUTT?

Baboons have rough, nerveless callouses (thick skin) on their bottoms so they can sit anywhere in total comfort!

DID YOU KNOW?

A woman found a lunch box in an Edinburgh street in 2006 and opened it to find it was full of baby boa constrictors. Snake sandwich, anyone?

WHICH CREATURE EATS ITS OWN SKIN?

Around four times a year, adult toads will shed their skin then eat it.

DO WE SWALLOW BUGS IN OUR SLEEP?

While sleeping, humans swallow an average of 14 bugs per year.

WHAT DO SPIDERS TASTE LIKE?

Fried spiders are regularly eaten as a delicacy in Cambodia. Apparently they taste like nuts.

DID YOU KNOW?

A female mosquito can drink one and a half times its own weight in blood in a single meal.

WHAT IS THE WORLD RECORD FOR EATING EARTHWORMS?

C. Manoharan of India set a new world record in 2003 by swallowing 200 live earthworms in just over 20 seconds.

WHICH ANIMAL CAN LICK ITS OWN EAR?

Giraffes have such long and flexible tongues that they can lick inside their own ears. Nobody knows what they taste like though.

DID YOU KNOW?

A hyena can chew a broken bottle without hurting itself.